BLACK INVENTORS

Black INVENTORS

★ 15 INVENTIONS THAT CHANGED THE WORLD ★

Kathy Trusty

Illustrations by Jerrard Polk

ROCKRIDGE PRESS

For general information on our other products and services or to obtain technical support, please contact our Customer Care Department within the United States at (866) 744-2665, or outside the United States at (510) 253-0500.

Rockridge Press publishes its books in a variety of electronic and print formats. Some content that appears in print may not be available in electronic books, and vice versa.

Cover and Interior Designer: Lindsey Dekker
Art Producer: Samantha Ulban
Editor: Barbara J. Isenberg
Production Editor: Rachel Taenzler
Production Manager: Michael Kay

ISBN: Print 978-1-64876-868-2 | eBook 978-1-64876-269-7
R0

Printed in China

Contents

Introduction

It is incredible how many things that people use and rely on every day started with someone wanting to solve a problem. And it is absolutely amazing how technology—which people don't even realize they are using—was developed because an inventor had an idea and was curious to see where that idea would lead.

Inventors are creative. They like to tinker and make things not only because they want a financial reward, but because they like to create and improve things. And for many inventors, that creative process started when they were young.

Over the years, great achievements have been made in science and technology. Black inventors have been responsible for many of those achievements and have created some of the greatest inventions the world has ever seen. Many of these Black inventors came from humble beginnings and faced many challenges. But as the inventor and engineer Mark Dean has said, "There may be obstacles, but there are no limits."

You will likely be amazed that some of the things in your home, things that you use every day but never really think about, were created by a Black inventor. This book features 15 of these inventors and their inventions. Some were problem solvers, while others were just curious. However, they all started with an idea and became great after seeing it through. You will learn their stories and the obstacles they had to overcome, and you will see how determined they were.

Take Lonnie Johnson, who was working on a heat pump and accidentally made one of the best-selling toys in the world. Then there is Marie Van Brittan Brown, who didn't feel safe in her home. She created her own home security system. You will also read about Elijah McCoy, who invented a way to apply oil to a moving train's engine so it could keep going and stay on schedule. And you will read about Sarah Goode, who invented a desk that folded out into a bed.

Most of the inventors featured in this book did not start with much more than an idea. If you have an idea and wonder if it makes sense, don't be discouraged. Keep thinking about it. Keep improving on it. Who knows? It could one day lead to a big invention.

Benjamin BANNEKER

{ 1731–1806 }

WOOD CLOCK *and* BANNEKER'S ALMANAC

Growing up, Benjamin Banneker had never seen a clock. Yet he made one out of wood that kept perfect time for more than 40 years. Later in life, he taught himself an advanced level of mathematics, and he learned astronomy by looking at the stars and studying them. He also gathered data and published an almanac, which is a book of facts and tables that predict the weather and other natural events. Benjamin's almanac was very popular and contained information that was helpful to farmers and navigators. He also worked as a surveyor and helped design the shape of the city that became Washington, DC. Benjamin is known as the "First Black Man of Science."

Benjamin was born free of slavery in Baltimore County, Maryland, on November 9, 1731. When he was a young boy, his family purchased a 100-acre tobacco farm where he lived most of his life. Benjamin started working on the farm with his parents at a young age. He went to school, but only for a few years. He learned reading and writing mainly from his grandmother who had come to America as an **indentured servant**. Benjamin was bright and intelligent. From an early age it was obvious he had the ability to understand complex math and science.

When Benjamin was 22 years old, he borrowed a pocket watch from a friend. He was curious about how it worked and studied its mechanical operation. He then used what he learned to build a clock. At that time, all watches and clocks were made in Europe. Metal was the main material used to make them. Benjamin did not have any metal. Instead, he hand carved every piece of the clock out of wood. The clock worked and kept the correct time for years. Benjamin's clock was the first wood clock made in the United States. People were fascinated by his invention and visited him just to get a look at it.

In 1771, a Quaker family named Ellicott moved near the Banneker's farm. Benjamin became friends with several members of the family. One member, George Ellicott, was a land surveyor who also had an interest in astronomy. He owned several science books and lunar charts, and let Benjamin borrow them. Lunar charts are mathematical tables used to determine the position of the moon in the sky. Benjamin studied the books and charts, and without help from anyone, taught himself advanced mathematics and learned about astronomy.

Benjamin had a sharp mind for science and mathematics, and he loved thinking about the natural world. In 1789, he forecast his first **solar eclipse**. Many well-known astronomers did not agree with his prediction. But Benjamin proved them wrong when the eclipse did occur.

When Andrew Ellicott, George's cousin and an engineer, was asked to map out the city that would become Washington, DC, the nation's capital, he hired Benjamin to assist him. Benjamin's calculations were used to design the city's boundaries.

After helping with the design of Washington, DC, Benjamin returned to his farm. There, he worked on putting together an **ephemeris** and other information for an annual almanac. He had been planning to produce an almanac ever since reading and studying the science books and lunar charts that were loaned to him. Banneker's almanac was published by northern **abolitionists** in 1791, and it contained important data and forecasts for the year 1792. The almanac was one of the first almanacs created in the United States.

Banneker's Almanac was very popular in New Jersey, Pennsylvania, Delaware, Maryland, Virginia, and North Carolina. The almanac included a weather table with weather projections for each month of the year, as well as tables that predicted **high tide** and **low tide**. Benjamin's almanac also included information on travel distances and mailing costs, and it predicted the times for sunrise and sunset.

The information included in *Banneker's Almanac* was extremely valuable for the economy and agriculture. Farmers relied on the almanacs to determine the best time for planting and harvesting their crops. Sailors relied on the almanacs to determine when to sail and when to dock their boats. Without almanacs, farmers and navigators had no way of knowing what the weather patterns would be in advance of planning for the next year.

During that period almanacs were not just used to predict the weather and provide other scientific information. They were sometimes used to express a person's opinion. Although he was born free, Benjamin spoke out against slavery and wrote anti-slavery articles for his almanac.

Benjamin did not see a difference between enslaved Black people wanting freedom and the colonies fighting for freedom from the British. He pointed that out in a letter he wrote to Thomas Jefferson on August 19, 1791. In his letter, Benjamin encouraged Jefferson to help abolish slavery. At the time, Jefferson was serving as Secretary of State under President George Washington and was an enslaver. Though Benjamin did not ask Jefferson to free those he held in slavery, he expressed his opinion that Jefferson was being a **hypocrite**. Benjamin also included a copy of his almanac for 1792 with his letter. In his response to Benjamin, Jefferson admitted that he had mixed feelings about slavery. He also praised Benjamin for his accomplishments.

Banneker's almanacs were read as far away as Europe, and Benjamin received high praise for them. But he was not always happy about that, because he was praised as a Black man with great knowledge and not simply as a man with great knowledge. Still, after reading *Banneker's Almanac* some white people began to see that intelligence had nothing to do with skin color. *Banneker's Almanac* was published for six years.

Benjamin died on his farm on October 9, 1806. During his funeral his house caught fire. Everything was destroyed, including the wood clock, which was still working and keeping the correct time.

Benjamin Banneker is mostly remembered for making a clock out of wood and helping design Washington, DC. However, his annual *Banneker's Almanac* was more valuable to the development of the country. They provided invaluable information that industries, such as farming, needed for growth and planning each year.

BRAINSTORM! How did Banneker's Almanac and other farmer's almanacs influence the lives of those living in the mid-Atlantic states where it was used?

EXPLORE MORE! To learn more about almanacs, visit the exhibit at University of Missouri-St. Louis Mercantile Library.

Elijah McCOY

{ 1844–1929 }

LUBRICATORS

Imagine taking a train to visit family and friends. Every few miles the train stops so an engineer can add oil to the engine. If you were traveling far, a trip that should take hours would take days. Now, imagine working on a train going city to city to deliver logs, coal, and other important items and having to stop the train every hour for maintenance. It would be tedious and time consuming. That's what life was like for train passengers and workers before Elijah McCoy's invention. Elijah was one of America's greatest inventors. He created an oil cup that automatically lubricated locomotive steam engines.

Elijah McCoy was born in Canada on May 2, 1844. His parents, George and Mildred, had been enslaved in Kentucky. They escaped slavery on the Underground Railroad and settled in Canada. At that time, Canada was under British rule. Elijah's father served in the British military. After his service he was given 160 acres of land in Colchester, a town in Ontario, Canada. That's where

Elijah was born. The family stayed in Canada until the end of the American Civil War. Then they moved back to the United States and lived in Ypsilanti, Michigan.

Elijah was an inquisitive boy and always tried to figure out how mechanical things worked. He would often take things apart, look at how they operated, and put them back together. His parents encouraged his interest and wanted him to learn more. They saved their money, and when Elijah was 15 years old they sent him to Edinburgh, Scotland, to study mechanical engineering.

After studying and working as an apprentice in Scotland for five years, Elijah returned to the United States ready to find a job and put his engineering skills to good use. Unfortunately, because of racism, no one would hire a Black man to work as an engineer. Elijah ended up working as a firefighter with the Michigan Central Railroad.

Elijah's work on the railroad included keeping the locomotive steam engines lubricated. Lubrication was important because as the parts of the machines rubbed together, they created friction and overheated. The lubrication kept the machine parts working smoothly. But in order to lubricate them, the locomotives had to completely shut down. Elijah thought that this process wasn't efficient and that shutting the engines down wasted a lot of time. He knew there had to be a better way to keep steam engines lubricated.

While continuing his work as a firefighter for the railroad company, Elijah began studying how train locomotives worked. He wanted to see if he could come up with a better way to apply lubrication. After studying their mechanics and how they operated, he created a device that would automatically lubricate the engines without having to completely shut them down. In 1872, Elijah obtained a patent for his invention, called "Improvement in Lubricators for Steam Engines." A patent protects the inventor from people stealing their idea and proves the invention is theirs.

Elijah's invention was a drip cup with a stem, valve, and spring that could be screwed into the area that required regular lubrication. As the train kept moving and the spring bounced up and down, oil would flow from the cup to parts of the engine that needed the oil.

Meanwhile, other companies that used large machinery for production had also been shutting down their equipment periodically to lubricate the machines. When they began using Elijah's invention, they no longer had to shut down machines and disrupt production. The machines could run continuously and receive necessary lubrication at the same time. This led to an overall increase in production.

Elijah did not stop after he invented the oil drip cup. He continued looking for ways to improve how machines were lubricated. He kept working and coming up with better versions to apply oil to steam engines, locomotives, and other machines. Elijah also worked as a consultant for manufacturing companies to make sure their engineers understood the proper way to install and use his lubricators.

Elijah also developed ways to enhance or improve common objects. In 1874, he obtained a patent for an improvement to the ironing board. His improvement kept the ironing board from moving back and forth when a person was ironing. In 1915, he received a patent for an invention that improved vehicle tires. Vehicle tires have grooves and treads. The grooves are the sunken part and the treads are the parts that touch the road. Elijah's improvement was to make the tread thicker, which helped cut down on how far tires would skid. When tires don't have tread, they can skid or slide, sometimes hitting another car or causing an accident.

Elijah also received patents for his designs. These included patents for a lawn sprinkler, a rubber heel for shoes, and an eraser. In total, he received more than 50 patents for his inventions. Most were for his lubricators. Many of the products he invented, however, never had his name on them. They were assigned to others because Elijah did not have the funds necessary to mass produce and sell the products.

In 1920, Elijah established the Elijah McCoy Manufacturing Company in Detroit, Michigan. He wanted to produce and sell lubricators that had his name on them. Two years later he was seriously injured in an automobile accident. He never fully recovered.

While Elijah invented a variety of products, his most impactful invention was his lubricator, the oil drip cup, and its many improved versions. That invention modernized the railroad industry and other industries that used large machinery. The oil cup that Elijah invented became a regular part on big machinery.

Over the years, other scientists and inventors tried to duplicate Elijah's lubricators, but none of these inventions worked as well as his. When buyers purchased large machinery for their companies, they would often ask if the machine had the "real McCoy." It's not certain if that expression comes directly from Elijah, but even today, that term is used to specify that something is real and not an imitation.

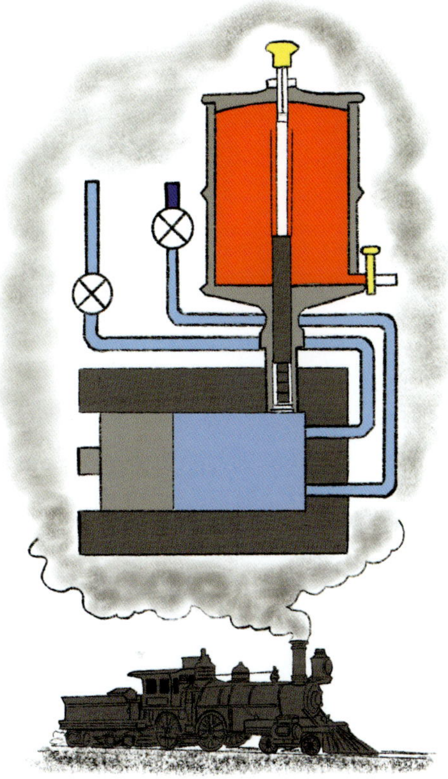

BRAINSTORM! Factories use large equipment to make goods that we consume every day. If there was no way to automatically lubricate machines, how would that affect production?

EXPLORE MORE! To learn about how locomotives work and more, visit the Railroad Museum of Pennsylvania at RRMuseumPA.org.

There are photographs on the internet supposedly of Sarah E. Goode, but they cannot be verified. Because we can't be sure what Sarah looked like, there is no illustration on this page.

Sarah E. GOODE

{ c. 1855–1905 }

CABINET BED

When people think about inventors they rarely think of women and are often surprised when they hear that women inventors came up with some of the things that make people's lives better. Many women are responsible for some of the comforts people enjoy in their homes today. So, the next time you visit a relative and you're offered a pullout sofa or a folding cot to sleep on, think about the inventor Sarah Goode. Sarah created a unique piece of furniture called a "cabinet bed" and became one of the first Black women in the United States to receive a patent for their invention.

Sarah Goode was born Sarah Elizabeth Jacob in Toledo, Ohio, sometime between 1850 and 1855. A few years after the Civil War ended, her family moved to Chicago, Illinois. Sarah's father worked as a carpenter, and her mother stayed home to take care of Sarah and her three siblings. Sarah attended school in Chicago, but how long she went and what grade she reached is

unknown. In 1880, she married Archibald Goode, who was a carpenter and stair builder.

Sarah became a business owner and opened a furniture store with Archibald. She was committed to making her customers happy and did what she could to fulfill any furniture needs they had. One particular problem caught her attention, and she focused on solving it.

Many of Sarah's customers lived in cramped apartments in the **working-class** section of Chicago. During this time it was common for **multigenerational** families to live together. Apartments in Chicago were very small and could not fit all the furniture a family needed to live comfortably. Even when they could afford the furniture they needed, families did not have the space for it. Sarah's customers often complained about that while they were shopping in her store. After hearing those complaints Sarah started working on a solution. Her solution was a folding bed, or hideaway bed.

Having grown up with a father who was a carpenter and being married to one, Sarah was very familiar with carpentry and building things. She used the knowledge she had gained from watching her father and husband and came up with an idea for a piece of furniture that could be a bed at night and a desk during the day.

Families could have more space when everyone was up and moving around.

Sarah invented a bed that would become a rolltop desk when folded up. Rolltop desks were a popular piece of furniture. They looked very nice and were found in many homes and offices. It's likely that Sarah chose that style because she was a businesswoman. Plus, rolltop desks were great for places that did not have a lot of space. They had a flexible cover that could be pulled down to cover the desktop or writing area and rolled up when someone needed to use it.

When Sarah's cabinet bed was folded, it looked just like a normal rolltop desk and had all the features of a regular desk. There was a writing area that parents could use to write letters and children could use to do their homework. It had drawers like a normal desk. It also had pigeonholes, which are small slots for storing things such as stationery, mail, and writing supplies. Sarah's invention was unique and extremely functional. And it was very good for small spaces.

Using her carpentry experience, Sarah was able to ensure that the bed could be lifted, folded, and unfolded without breaking apart or damaging the desk. She also included extra support under the bed's center part when it was unfolded, so it would not sag in the middle.

On July 18, 1885, Sarah received a patent for her folding cabinet bed. It was not easy in those days for a Black inventor to obtain a patent, but Sarah remained determined. She had been working on her invention since 1883.

Over the years, cabinet beds became more and more popular. Like Sarah's cabinet bed, they were designed to be used as another piece of furniture. Other inventors had some success with variations on the hideaway, too. In 1911, the Murphy bed was invented for the same reason that Sarah created her cabinet bed. People needed furniture for small living spaces. The Murphy bed began as a bed that was pushed up and into a wall when not being used. Then, later versions of the Murphy bed became more like Sarah's version. When not being used as a bed, they became a cabinet or wall shelf. Even IKEA, the Swedish furniture store, created a cabinet bed in the 1950s that looked remarkably similar to Sarah's invention.

Regardless, Sarah's invention was the **forerunner** for hideaway beds. Even though similar inventions by others have become more popular and are being used today, Sarah Goode deserves the credit for being one of the first people in the United States to create a piece of **multipurpose** furniture.

BRAINSTORM! Sarah's cabinet-bed invention did not have as much success as the Murphy bed. Why do you think that was?

EXPLORE MORE! To learn more about furniture and how it has been made and decorated for over 600 years visit the Victoria & Albert Museum in London, or through their website, VaM.ac.uk.

Lyda NEWMAN

{ c. 1885–? }

IMPROVED HAIRBRUSH

There was a time when owning a hairbrush was considered a luxury. It was an expensive item that only the wealthy could afford and were not found in most homes, especially in Black homes. Most hairbrushes were hand carved. When they became a little more affordable, they were still not suited for the texture of Black hair.

Today the hairbrush is a common item, and many are designed to manage the texture of Black women's hair. One reason for that is the invention from Lyda Newman, who at the age of 14 designed an improvement to the hairbrush. Her improvement made it cheaper to make and even more affordable. Lyda made a great contribution to the hair industry, yet very little is known about her, and she has not received much recognition for that contribution.

Lyda was born in Ohio in 1885. Her father was a steel-worker and her mother was a homemaker. Her parents were very supportive of her and wanted her to have opportunities for a better life. By the time she was a teenager, Lyda had moved to New York City and was living on her own.

Lyda had always styled her own hair and her friends' hair. In New York, she soon started working as a hairdresser. She worked for a family as a private hairdresser. But Lyda was disappointed in the tools she had to work with, especially the hairbrushes. She could not find what she needed because the brushes that were available were not effective on Black women's hair texture. What worked for one hair type did not necessarily work on a different hair type.

If Lyda wanted to provide the best service possible to her clients, she would need better tools to work with. Since she couldn't purchase what she needed, she decided that she would have to create a different kind of brush.

In those days, hairbrushes were very fragile. The bristles were made of animal hair, often from horses, which made them expensive and difficult to clean and maintain. Hairdressers had to wash and dry the brushes by hand before and after each client. The brush that Lyda invented had several unique features. Her invention was durable and affordable. It had **synthetic** bristles instead of bristles made from animal hair. That feature alone made it more affordable.

Lyda's brush was also more hygienic. It consisted of two parts that could be snapped together. One part was the base of the brush and the handle. The other part had the bristles attached to it. In order to connect the two parts, you had to slide the part with the bristles over the base and snap it into place. There were tiny holes in the section that held the bristles. When the two parts were snapped together it created a hollow area underneath the bristles.

When hair was being brushed, debris such as dandruff would fall through the little holes into the hollow area. That made cleaning the brush easy. You just pulled the brush apart, emptied the hollow area, and washed the two parts. The most important feature was that her brush was easy to manufacture. Lyda received a patent for her "Improved Brush" on November 15, 1898.

In addition to being an inventor and improving hair care for Black women, Lyda was a women's rights activist. She was active in the suffrage movement in New York. The suffrage movement was the fight to win the right to vote for women. And though the activists agreed on the goal, the Black and white suffragists sometimes had differing approaches. Some white suffragist organizations excluded Black women, while others accepted Black women but were not fully welcoming. For example, if they were marching in a parade, sometimes the Black women were told to march in the back.

Nevertheless, Lyda worked right alongside the well-known white suffragists of the day. She was very involved in activism around New York. Lyda organized gatherings to bring women together to discuss the importance of voting and having that right. She was also

the cofounder of the African-American branch of the Woman Suffrage Party.

The Woman Suffrage Party fought for **enfranchisement** of women living in New York. It was a political union that brought all the suffrage organizations in the state together. Their goal was to get a women's suffrage amendment added to the New York State Constitution.

The work of suffragists in states around the country led to ratification of the 19th Amendment. The 19th Amendment gave American women in all states the right to vote. It was added to the federal constitution and ratified on August 18, 1920. However, the right to vote was not applied equally to everyone. Even though the amendment included women of color, many of them were still unable to vote because of voting restrictions like **poll**

taxes and **literacy tests**. It wasn't until the Voting Rights Act of 1965 that full voting rights for Black women—and men—were put into practice.

Lyda is remembered for her contributions to Black hair care as well as her activism. And though it is not clear if they were inspired by Lyda, others began creating hair care products specifically for Black women.

Annie Turnbo Malone, for instance, developed a product that stimulated hair growth. In 1918, she founded Poro College, a school that taught women how to nourish and style Black hair. One of the women that worked for Annie, Madam C. J. Walker, also invented hair care products for Black women and became a successful and well-known businesswoman. Through the years, many more products and tools were developed for Black women. Today the Black hair care business is a $1.2 trillion business and growing.

BRAINSTORM! Black women were fighting for voting rights and civil rights at the same time. How do you think the two are related?

EXPLORE MORE! To learn about Black leaders in the women's suffrage movement visit the Turning Point Suffragist Memorial at SuffragistMemorial.org.

George Washington CARVER

{ c. 1864–1943 }

SCIENTIST, INVENTOR OF PRODUCTS FROM PEANUTS

George Washington Carver did not go to school until he was 11 years old, yet he is known as one of America's greatest educators. A wise teacher convinced him to study science and agriculture. That decision put George on the path to becoming one of America's greatest scientists, inventors, educators, and researchers. He convinced southern farmers to plant peanuts. When there was a surplus, and the farmers were struggling to sell them, he helped the farmers by developing more than 300 ways to use the crops. People called him the "Peanut Man."

George was born in 1864 during the Civil War. He was an enslaved person, living on a farm owned by Moses and Susan Carver in Diamond Grove, Missouri. Enslaved persons did not get birth certificates, so George never knew his exact date of birth. He only knew that he was born sometime between 1864 and 1865.

When George was a baby, he and his mother were kidnapped from the Carver farm by slave raiders who were hoping to sell them for profit in a neighboring state. Moses was able to get George back by trading his prize horse for his release. He was not able to get George's mother back, and George never saw her again.

The Carvers raised George, and Susan taught him how to read and write. George spent a lot of time with Susan in her garden. He enjoyed working with plants. He began experimenting with the soil and became very good at helping the plants grow. He even helped local farmers who had trouble making things in their garden grow. The farmers started calling him the "plant doctor."

At the age of 11, George left the Carver farm and went to a city called Neosho, in Missouri, where there was a school for Black students. George attended the school for a couple of years before leaving. This was during a period when many Black people were moving to the west for a better life. George ended up in Kansas, where he graduated from high school. After high school, George was accepted at Highland College, an all-white school. But when he showed up at Highland the school's administrator turned him away because he was Black.

After his experience at Highland, George worked on a farm for several years. George still enjoyed working with plants and experimenting with them. He also liked to paint. In 1890, he enrolled in Simpson College in

Indianola, Iowa, to study art and piano. He was hesitant to apply at first because of what happened with Highland. Soon, though, people around George noticed his talent and interest in plants. One of his art teachers at Simpson advised him to attend Iowa State Agricultural School and study botany. Botany is the scientific study of plants.

By the time George graduated from Iowa State, his work with plants and his research on plants was well known. Schools from around the world wanted him to come work for them, but George wanted his work and knowledge to benefit Black farmers. He accepted an offer to lead the agricultural department at Tuskegee Institute, a college for Black people in Tuskegee, Alabama. In addition to teaching classes and conducting research in his lab, George worked with local Black farmers. He wanted them to understand the science behind farming.

Cotton was then the main agricultural crop in Alabama. But production had dropped, and the farmers did not understand why. They were doing what they always did, yet the fields were not producing as much as before. George introduced the farmers to a new planting system called crop rotation.

When you plant the same crop in the same spot year after year, the soil loses the nutrients needed to make the crops grow. George taught the farmers to switch up what they planted. Instead of planting cotton every year, he had them plant crops such as peanuts, soybeans, or sweet potatoes. Those were easier to grow, and they restored nitrogen, a soil nutrient, to the ground. Rotating the crops

would also give the soil time to replenish other nutrients, so cotton would grow again.

That system worked and the soil improved. But the farmers found that they had more peanuts than they could consume or sell. So George went back to his lab and began experimenting and developing ways to use the excess peanuts.

George discovered that peanuts could be used to create hundreds of products. Many of them are food products that people consume almost every day. Some of the food items George developed from peanuts are milk, cream, cheese, instant coffee, sauce, and cooking oil. George also believed that non-food products could be developed from agricultural products. In 1925, he received a patent for the development of a face cream made from peanuts. Through his many experiments he also discovered that peanuts could be used to make paper, plastic, linoleum, dye, and wood stains.

While George is best known for his experiments with peanuts and the many ways they can be used or consumed, he also conducted research on other agricultural products. He discovered that sweet potatoes could be used to make tapioca, molasses, vinegar, ink, paint, and dye. During World War I, George worked with Henry Ford, the automobile manufacturer, to develop synthetic rubber out of peanuts for the military.

In 1921, George spoke before Congress in support of the Peanut Grower's Association. The growers were fighting to have a tariff imposed to keep imported peanuts out of the country. George's testimony helped get the tariff passed. The United States is now the third-largest producer of peanuts in the world. George's work and experiments had a huge impact on the peanut industry.

BRAINSTORM! How have some of the products that George Washington Carver created from peanuts made your life better?

EXPLORE MORE! To learn more about the experiments George Washington Carver conducted at Tuskegee Institute, visit a digital exhibit of George's work at the United States Department of Agriculture: NAL.USDA.gov/exhibits/ipd/carver.

Garrett MORGAN

{ 1877–1963 }

SAFETY MASK *and* TRAFFIC SIGNAL

When you see traffic lights that stay red in both directions for a few seconds, that's because of Garrett Morgan. When you see firefighters wearing masks that keep them from suffocating when they rush into buildings to save those inside, that's because of Garrett Morgan. Garrett Morgan was known for two things: He was a successful businessman, and he was a great inventor.

Garrett did not have many advantages growing up, but he did not let that stop him. He was motivated and worked to make a better life for himself. He was born in Paris, Kentucky, on March 4, 1877, the seventh of 11 children. The period that followed the Civil War, known as the Reconstruction era, was just ending. Both of his parents, Elizabeth and Sydney, had been enslaved. Elizabeth was of Indigenous and African descent and was the daughter of a Baptist minister. Sydney was the son of John Hunt Morgan, a Confederate colonel.

Garrett did not have much education. He went to elementary school but only to the sixth grade. He left home when he was 14 years old and moved to Cincinnati, Ohio. In Cincinnati, he found work as a handyman. He was eventually able to hire a tutor so he could continue learning.

In 1895, Garrett moved to Cleveland. There he found work as a sewing machine repairman for a clothing company. Garrett was the only Black repairman with the company. He learned as much as he could about sewing machines and understood how they worked. Garrett saved his earnings and in 1907 opened his own repair shop.

Garrett did not stop at owning one business. In 1909, he opened a tailoring shop. He designed most of the machines used in the shop. At one point he had more than 30 people working for him. He also developed a hair straightening cream, and in 1913 established the G. A. Morgan Hair Refining Company. In 1920, he started the *Cleveland Call*, a newspaper that printed news stories that were important to the Black community. He also opened an all-Black country, or community, club. Garrett's businesses were successful, and he became a wealthy man. That success made it possible for him to finance the inventions he was working on.

In 1914, Garrett invented a breathing device. The device was a hood with an attached tube that would fit over a person's head. The tube was long enough to extend through a room filled with thick smoke to the cleaner air near the floor, where it was fresher. The device, which was called a safety hood, was developed to benefit firefighters. They could breathe freely when they entered a house or building filled with smoke or poisonous gas. Although designed mainly for firefighters, the breathing devices also provided protection to chemists, engineers, and other workers who found themselves working around dangerous fumes and dust particles. Garrett later updated his invention to include a mouthpiece.

Garrett's breathing device was badly needed, but it did not gain popularity until two years later when there was an explosion that trapped workers in a tunnel. In July 1916, men were working on a tunnel under Lake Erie near Cleveland, Ohio. A sudden gas explosion trapped more than 20 men under mud and rocks. Attempts to rescue the workers failed, and many of the rescuers were injured or killed. Garrett heard about the accident. He went to the area with his newly invented breathing devices. The rescue workers, led by Garrett and wearing his safety hood, were able to go deep into the tunnel and bring out the survivors and the bodies of those who had died.

The rescue was a significant feat, and newspapers wrote stories about it. But Garrett, the Black man who led the rescue, was not mentioned. Instead, the papers focused on the safety hoods the rescuers wore. Though Garrett did not get any credit for the rescue, he began to get a lot of requests for his safety hood.

Garrett gave many presentations on his safety hood and how it worked. At that time, America was

racially segregated, and Black people were not welcomed by white people in many areas. It would even have been dangerous for Garrett to claim the invention was his. Often when Garrett was asked to give a presentation, he would hire a white actor to pretend to be the inventor. Garrett would pose as the assistant.

The success of Garrett's business made it possible for him to buy an automobile. He was the first Black person in Cleveland to own one. One day while driving he saw an accident between a horse-drawn buggy and an automobile. He realized that, as more and more people bought cars, safety would become an issue. After seeing the accident, Garrett went to work on finding a solution to make it safer for automobile traffic and for people crossing the street.

In 1922, he made an improvement to the traffic signal. His improvement was the addition of an indicator that would stop traffic in all directions. Before Garrett's invention, automobiles and other vehicles would often collide in the middle of the intersection. The traffic signal would go directly from red to green or green to red, with no pause in between. Vehicles would get stuck in the intersection, and pedestrians would not have enough time to cross the street. Garrett's improvement gave the traffic light three signals. It had a signal for go, a second signal for stop, and a third signal for all cars in both directions to stop. Garrett's improvement gave vehicles time to clear the intersection, and it gave pedestrians time to get to the other side of the street.

Garrett received a patent for his traffic signal in 1923. He later sold the patent for his invention to the General Electric Company. Even today, traffic signals are modeled after Garrett's invention. But while Garrett is best known for his improvement to the traffic signal, his greatest invention, and the most far-reaching, was the safety hood. Garrett's hood with the long tube became the forerunner to the gas mask.

Once the effectiveness of Garrett's safety hood became known, fire departments and other rescue operations became customers. It was sought out by the United States military and was used as the model for the gas masks that were used during World War I. He also received orders for his product from fire departments and mine owners across Europe.

Gas masks are now used in numerous industries to protect people from smoke, poisonous gases, and other harmful chemicals. They are used by law enforcement, **first responders**, and in hospitals and factories. The idea behind the technology used in the production of gas masks today stems from the safety hood invented by Garrett.

BRAINSTORM! How dangerous would it be if there was no yellow light to warn drivers that the light is getting ready to turn red?

EXPLORE MORE! To learn about the history of cars and to see Garrett Morgan's early traffic signal, visit the Smithsonian National Museum of American history in Washington, DC, or at AmericanHistory.SI.edu.

Charles DREW

{ 1904–1950 }

BLOOD BANK

When people are sick or injured, they sometimes need blood to help them heal or get better. When someone is having an operation, having extra blood in the hospital operating room can be a life saver. But, in order to have blood available to help patients, it needs to be stored a certain way to make it safe to be reused. Dr. Charles Drew, a pioneer in blood research, figured out how to do that. He called the blood he stored "banked blood." Charles is now known as the "father of the blood bank."

Charles was born in Washington, DC, on June 3, 1904. His father, Richard, was a carpet layer and the only Black member of his local **labor union**. His mother, Nora, had attended Miner Teachers College but never worked as a teacher. Education was important to the Drew family, and Charles and his three younger siblings were encouraged to take it seriously. They were also encouraged to be independent and responsible. When Charles was 12 years old he made money selling newspapers. He was determined and hired other boys to work for him, so he could sell papers to more people.

Charles was an average student in high school, but he excelled in sports. He graduated from high school in 1922 and received an athletic scholarship to Amherst College in Massachusetts. Charles was a star athlete in college. He enjoyed sports and he began to excel in some of his classes, particularly biology. Then, two things happened that made him interested in becoming a doctor—he was hurt while playing football and had to spend time in a hospital, and his older sister, who had **tuberculosis**, died.

After Charles graduated from Amherst in 1926, he went to medical school. He graduated at the top of his class from McGill University School of Medicine in Canada. Charles stayed in Canada to complete his residency, the period of training after medical school. It was there that he became interested in **transfusion medicine** and blood transfusions from person to person.

A few years later, while working towards an advanced science degree at Columbia University in New York, Charles began his research on storing and preserving blood. Blood is made up of several parts, and one of those parts is plasma. He discovered that the plasma in blood could be saved, and if stored correctly could be used for blood transfusions into other patients.

This was an important discovery because when blood is removed from a person it quickly loses its usefulness.

If a patient needs blood immediately, often there is a scramble to find a relative or friend who can donate blood so the patient can be saved. But what if blood could be accumulated and stored and ready when a patient needs it? Charles's discovery was immediately important for the many lives it could save.

Charles experimented with his discovery and created a blood bank in a New York hospital. A blood bank is a place where blood donations are kept. Blood that is donated is first examined to determine which type it is and to make sure it is safe to be used in a transfusion. Then, its parts are separated and safely put away until it is needed for a patient. A doctor who Charles worked with invented a container that blood could be stored in. He gave it to Charles, so he could use it in the work he was doing with blood storage.

By 1940, Charles had become the leading expert on storing blood for transfusions. During World War II, as the fighting in Europe increased, the US and its allies desperately needed extra blood to save soldiers' lives. Charles led a British program called the Blood for Britain Project. The organization collected thousands of pints of plasma and set up blood banks in Europe to store it. Charles was later asked to establish blood banks for the American Red Cross, so blood would be available when American soldiers needed it.

During this time, he introduced the bloodmobile. This effort allowed people to make blood donations at places outside of hospitals and medical facilities. Companies, organizations, and their workers could easily give blood for the military. Trained medical staff would go from place to place, collect blood from participants, and take it to blood banks to be examined and stored. The blood-mobiles greatly increased the amount of blood that was collected and stored to avoid shortages, even when war or major disasters caused many injuries and increased the need for transfusions.

As the war progressed, the need for blood increased. Black people were not allowed to donate blood. Charles protested and in 1942 the military ruled that Black people would be allowed to donate blood but it would be stored separately. Charles disagreed with that ruling, and he left the American Red Cross. As a scientist, Charles knew there was no difference between blood from a Black person and blood from a white person. People have different blood types, but the difference is based on other factors and not a person's race. Charles's departure from the Red Cross did not lessen the value of his work. Developing a way to save and store blood was a great contribution to science.

Blood transfusions are crucial during surgery and for patients suffering from traumatic injuries. Transfusions are also critical in the treatment of chronic illnesses such as cancer. According to the American Red Cross, a person is in need of a blood transfusion every two seconds, and every time there is an automobile accident there could be a need for about 100 units of blood. One unit is 17.75 ounces. About 6.8 million people in the United

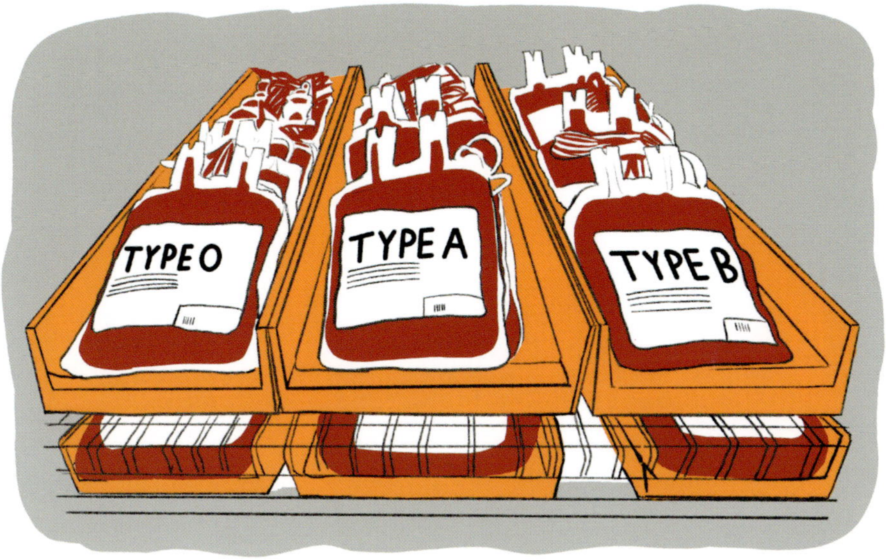

States donate blood every year. One donation can save up to three lives.

BRAINSTORM! Why is it important to know your blood type?

EXPLORE MORE! To learn more about Charles Drew and other science innovations, visit the Science History Institute in Philadelphia or at ScienceHistory.org.

Bessie Blount GRIFFIN

{ 1914–2009 }

FEEDING APPARATUS

When Bessie Blount Griffin was seven, her teacher punished her for writing with her left hand by striking her knuckles. Bessie quietly rebelled by teaching herself to write with both hands, her feet, and even her teeth. Years later that rebellion helped her in her work with wounded soldiers when they returned home from fighting in World War II. Many of the soldiers returned paralyzed or as **amputees**. Bessie, who was a physical therapist, was there to help them.

Bessie did not have any special equipment, but she had a lot of ideas. She was very creative, imaginative, and resourceful. The wounded soldiers had to learn a new way of doing things, and Bessie worked with them. She wanted to help them maintain their independence by changing how they performed basic tasks. Bessie was a great scientist and inventor.

Bessie was born in Hickory, Virginia, on November 24, 1914. She attended Diggs Chapel Elementary School, which was established after the Civil War to educate Black children. Bessie was forced to stop her elementary education in the sixth grade. Her family later moved to New Jersey where Bessie earned her GED. A GED is a General Education Diploma for those who did not graduate from high school. In order to get a GED Bessie had to take a test to show that she had high school-level academic skills.

After receiving her GED, Bessie studied nursing at Kenney Memorial Hospital in New Jersey. This was one of the first hospitals in New Jersey to train Black doctors and nurses. She soon became interested in physical therapy, which was a new profession at the time. Physical therapy is the treatment of disease and injury by physical means, such as exercise and massage instead of drugs. Bessie later attended Panzer College of Physical Education and became a licensed physical therapist. She was one of the first physical therapists in the country.

Bessie began her physical therapy career working at the Bronx Hospital in New York City. The hospital served World War II veterans, many of whom had returned home severely wounded. Bessie worked mostly with those who were paralyzed or amputees. She refused to let them give up. If they complained about being a person with disabilities, Bessie would tell them to change their mindset. She helped them get used to using **assistive technology**, so they wouldn't have to rely on others.

Bessie remembered how she had taught herself to write without using her hands. For the veterans whose arms had been amputated, she taught them how to use their feet to do the things they once did with their hands. Then, one day, a doctor mentioned that what the paralyzed veterans and amputees really needed was a way to feed themselves. Bessie began to work on creating a device that would serve that need. She turned her apartment into a lab and spent months working on a design. She was committed to the project and used her own money to buy what she needed. It took almost a year, but she finally had an apparatus that amputees and those suffering from paralysis could use to feed themselves.

On April 24, 1951, Bessie received a patent for her invention. She called it a portable receptacle support. Her invention was a device that could be worn around the neck. It consisted of a tube that would be attached to a cup or bowl. When patients bit down on the tube, bite-sized portions of food would be delivered to their mouth. The device shut off automatically to avoid overfeeding or choking the person. When they were ready for another bite of food, they would bite down on the tube again. Bessie's invention gave patients the ability to feed themselves while remaining in an upright position.

Bessie was excited about her device, and when she demonstrated it audiences loved it. She was sure the Veterans Administration would love it as well because it would give veterans a level of independence. But when Bessie presented her device to the Veterans Administration they rejected it. She was told that it was impractical and that patients were better off being fed by nurses and other hospital staff. Bessie tried everything she could think of to get the government to see how important her invention was. She even went on a television show called *The Big Ideas* to demonstrate it. She was the first woman and first Black person to appear on the show.

After having her device rejected by the United States government and the Veterans Administration, she sold the idea to the French government. The French happily bought it and started using it in their military hospitals throughout their country. Bessie later invented a disposable cardboard vomit basin. Vomit basins, known as emesis basins, are used in hospitals at a patient's bedside for bodily fluids. Disposable basins are more sanitary and hygienic. Once again, the United States government was not interested. The government of Belgium bought the idea and it soon became a standard in their hospitals.

While Bessie was disappointed that her ideas were not accepted in the United States, she continued working as a nurse and physical therapist. She began to notice changes in her patients' handwriting as they progressed in their physical therapy. She conducted research on medical graphology, which is the study of handwriting and its relationship to a person's personality. Bessie turned her interest toward **forensic science**. She started a new career as a handwriting expert.

Hospitals in the United States now use disposable kidney-shaped bowls, but they are used more for other medical waste than for vomit. Their use has increased over the years because they are more sanitary than reusable

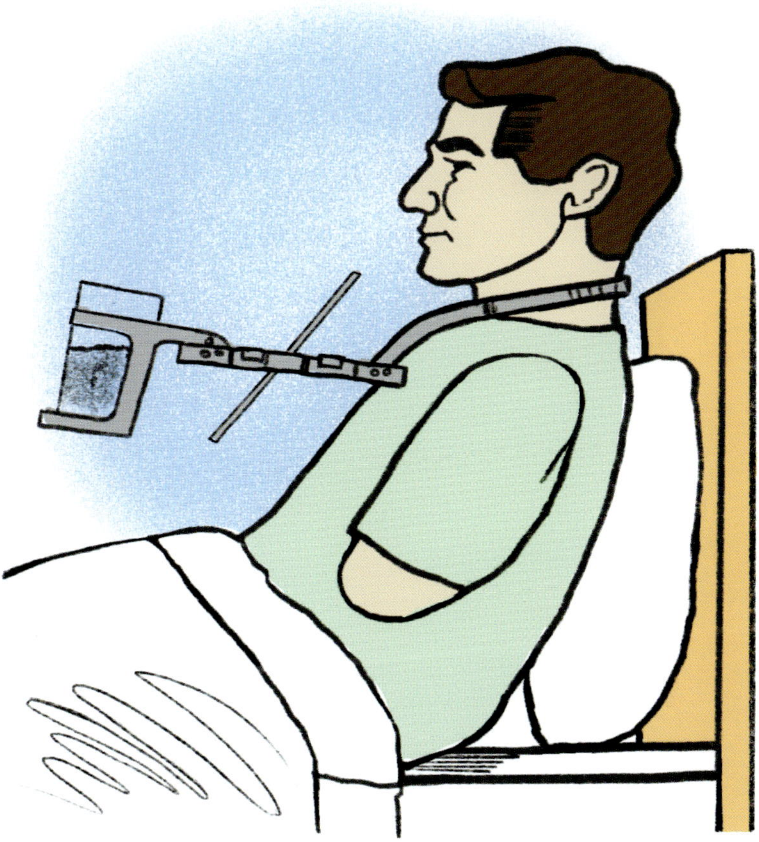

bowls, and they reduce the spread of infections. Although Bessie introduced the world to disposable medical containers, she never fully received credit for her invention.

Even though her portable feeding apparatus was never utilized in the United States, her contribution to medicine has been recognized. A couple of years after she developed her portable receptacle support, another person invented one. When he applied for a patent for his improved feeding apparatus, he referenced Bessie's invention on his application. He was not the only one. Over the years at least 20 patent applications for assistive technology have referenced Bessie's invention.

BRAINSTORM! What piece of assistive technology do you think you could improve? What would the improvement be?

EXPLORE MORE! To learn more about different types of assistive technology, visit the Assistive Technology Industry Association at ATIA.org.

Marie Van Brittan BROWN

{ 1922–1999 }

HOME SECURITY SYSTEM

After working long hours as a nurse, all Marie Van Brittan Brown wanted to do was go home and relax. But that was not always possible. Marie lived in a neighborhood that had a lot of crime. Also, her husband, Albert, had a job that took him away from home at night, leaving Marie home alone. Marie knew she had to do something if she wanted to feel safe at night and get a good night's sleep. She created the first home video security system that could remotely lock and unlock the door.

Not much is known about Marie's family and her early life. Her father was from Massachusetts, and her mother was from Pennsylvania. Marie was born in Jamaica, Queens, New York, in October 1922. She resided in New York City until her death in 1999.

Nurses, like most health-care providers, do not always work regular hours or the same hours every day. There were times when Marie worked during the day and returned home when it was still daylight. There were other times when she had to work in the evening and did not get home until late at night. Marie's husband, Albert, also worked different hours and shifts. Sometimes when Marie got home from work Albert would not be there or would be leaving for his job.

When Marie was resting or sleeping, she would often be disturbed by a commotion outside. If someone knocked on her door she was afraid to open it, because she could not see who was on the other side. She couldn't tell if it was one person or several people. She couldn't tell if it was someone who needed help or if it was someone trying to get in to cause trouble. It was horrible being afraid in her own home.

When things got really noisy or if she thought someone was getting hurt, she would call the police. But they did not always come right away. Marie reached a breaking point and decided if she wanted to feel safe and secure in her own home, she had to do something about it herself.

With the help of Albert, who was an electronics technician, Marie designed a security system that she described as a "Home Security System Utilizing Television Surveillance." Marie's system was extremely detailed and sophisticated for that time. It was in the 1960s, and no one had ever invented anything like it.

Marie's system was designed specifically to provide security for people living in a house or an apartment. It had two devices that would be strategically placed, depending on what the home or apartment owner needed.

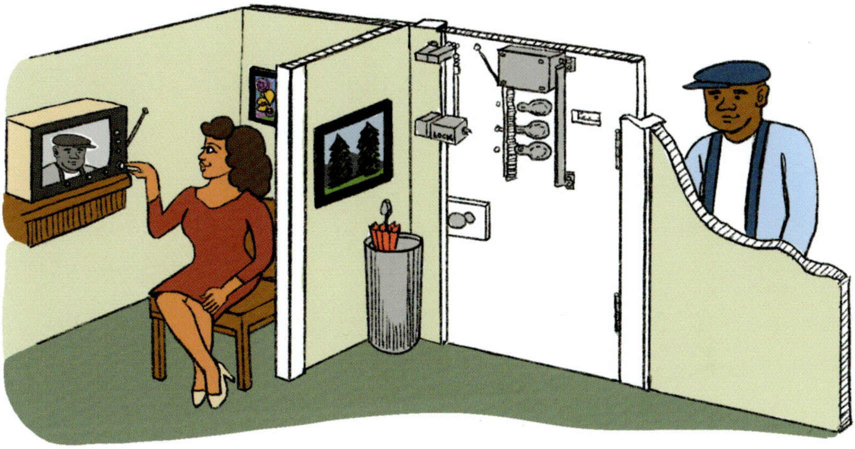

One device would be mounted at or near the entrance of the home. The other device, which was the control device, would be mounted in a room inside the home. Any room would work, including the bedroom if that's where the owner wanted it. The system was designed with audio and video that could be controlled remotely by the person inside the home.

Marie's home security system had several features that were revolutionary at the time. The video feature, which was actually the first **closed-circuit TV**, would scan the entrance of the home. It could be switched from stationary to movable. The person inside the home could look at one specific area, like at the door. Or, the viewer could use the movable feature and set the video-scanning device to automatically point in different directions in order to look at a wider area around the entrance. The person inside the home could also use the audio feature and speak with anyone at the door. They could record the conversation if they felt it was necessary. If it was someone they knew and wanted to let in they could release the lock by pressing a button on the device, without walking to the door. This was the first time a person was able to open a door by remote control.

Marie's security system also had an optional radio-controlled alarm. If the occupant of the home felt that they were in danger, they could activate the alarm, and a security station would be notified. The security station would then have access to the system's audio and video. The person at the security station would be able to see and question the person at the door and work with the occupant to determine if the situation was threatening.

Marie's system was so **groundbreaking** that the *New York Times*, one of the nation's most-read newspapers, wrote an article about the invention and printed it in their December 6, 1969, edition. Marie even received an award from the National Scientists Committee.

It is unclear if Marie made any money from her invention. What is clear is that her invention was the forerunner to the home security systems that are used today. Security systems that followed included many of the features of Marie's invention. Video monitoring, remote controls, and alert systems to notify the police or a security office are now commonplace in most systems today. And though Marie's system was created for the home, it became the model for systems that are used in buildings all around the country—banks, office buildings, small businesses, churches, schools, apartment buildings, grocery stores, and even the local drugstore.

Inventors in more than 30 patent applications for security systems have mentioned Marie's invention, and many inventors have included some of the same features that Marie had in her system. Today the home security industry is a billion-dollar business. Marie may not have received any great financial benefit for her invention, but her home security system was the first, and it is one of the reasons many people are able to feel safe and secure in their homes and in their workplaces today.

BRAINSTORM! Which features in Marie's security system are part of the system in the school you attend? Which feature would you like to have included in your school's system?

EXPLORE MORE! To see a collection of historic security alarms and learn about the security industry, visit the Security Museum in Lynn, Massachusetts, or online at WayneAlarm.com/antiques-corner.

Patricia BATH

{ 1942–2019 }

LASERPHACO EYE SURGERY DEVICE

When Patricia Bath was a high school student she was featured in the *New York Times*, a newspaper that is read worldwide, for helping to write a paper on a cancer study. At the age of just 16, she started winning awards for her scientific research. Patricia was an excellent student in high school and later in college. It is not at all surprising that she would be included in a *Time* magazine list of women who changed the world or that she would be the first Black female doctor to receive a patent for inventing a medical device.

Patricia was born in Harlem, New York, on November 4, 1942. Her father, who had emigrated from Trinidad in the Caribbean, worked for the New York City subway system. Her mother was a housekeeper. Patricia had two brothers—Rupert, whom she grew up with, and Ronald, who grew up in Trinidad. Patricia did not meet Ronald until she was an adult.

Patricia was always curious about science as a child. When her mother gave her a chemistry set she became even more interested in it and all that science could do.

In high school Patricia was at the top of her class. One summer she participated in a science program at Yeshiva University, where she studied the impact of stress and nutrition on cancer. After high school she attended Hunter College in New York, and she continued to excel. She graduated from Hunter in 1964 with a bachelor's degree in chemistry. She then went to medical school at Howard University, a historically Black college in Washington, DC.

After medical school Patricia returned to New York and completed her medical training at Harlem Hospital and Columbia University. She had decided to focus on ophthalmology, the study of the eye, its diseases, and treatment. Patricia completed her **residency** at New York University, where she became the school's first Black ophthalmology resident.

Training at Harlem Hospital and Columbia University was like training in two different **socioeconomic** worlds. Patricia noticed that patients at an eye clinic in Harlem seemed to be in much worse condition than patients at Columbia. The mostly Black patients in Harlem were blind or nearly blind, while the mostly white patients at Columbia were not. Patricia conducted a study and found that the occurrence of blindness in Black people was twice that of blindness in whites. She also determined that the high rate of blindness among Black

Americans was due to a lack of eye care. Patricia set out to change that.

Patricia came up with the idea of community ophthalmology. Community ophthalmology aims to prevent blindness as a part of regular health care. It applies the same methods that are used in public health and community health. As part of community ophthalmology, workers go into schools, community centers, and other places where health care is inadequate. They are trained to conduct annual eye examinations, which can catch eye diseases before they progress to blindness. Community ophthalmology is now practiced around the world.

In 1977, Patricia and two colleagues founded the American Institute for the Prevention of Blindness. They believed that eyesight is a basic human right and were dedicated to protecting, preserving, and restoring the gift of sight.

Throughout her career Patricia conducted ophthalmology research. In 1980, she began researching the use of laser techniques in eye care and surgery. The next year, she traveled to Berlin, Germany, to learn as much as she could about laser technology. A few years later she developed a method and device to remove cataracts.

Cataracts are like a cloud over the lens of the eye. They block out light and affect the person's vision. Cataracts normally occur in people over the age of 60. If a person suffers from an eye injury, however, cataracts may appear earlier. If cataracts are not removed a person could go blind. Cataracts are the leading cause of blindness in the United States, and surgery is required to remove them. The early surgery techniques were often risky and painful.

Patricia began giving thought to a device that would safely and efficiently remove cataracts. It took her five years to complete and test her invention to make sure it was safe and effective. Finally, the device that she invented was more advanced than any technology for eye care that was previously available. In 1988, Patricia received a patent for a surgical instrument, which she called a Laserphaco Probe, and another for her new method of removing cataracts.

Before Patricia's invention, doctors removed cataracts by making a three-millimeter incision in the eye and inserting a sharp instrument to break up the cataract lens and suction it out. With Patricia's technique the incision in the eye was much smaller, just one millimeter or less.

Then, the Laserphaco Probe is inserted, and radiation is used to break up the cataract. After the cataract is broken up, liquid is applied to flush it out, and a replacement lens is inserted. The radiation from the Laserphaco Probe breaks up the lens into finer particles, making the flushing process gentler.

Patricia's technique of using a laser in the removal of cataracts made cataract surgery faster, easier, and less invasive. Her invention was one of the most important developments in the field of ophthalmology. With her technique and the Laserphaco Probe, Patricia was able to restore the sight of patients who had been blind for years. She said that her greatest moment came when she restored sight to a woman in North Africa who had been blind for 30 years.

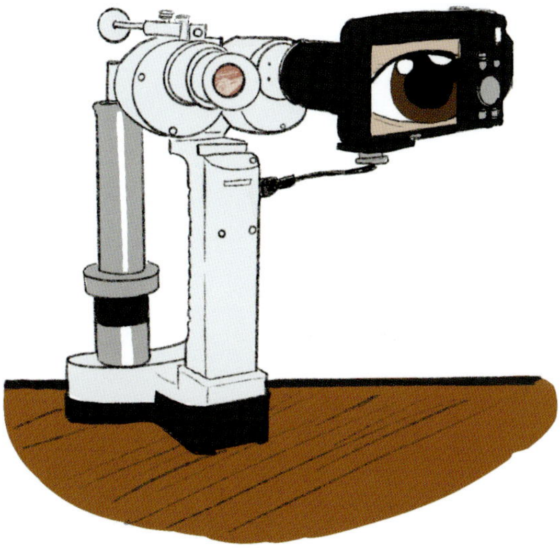

Patricia received five patents from the United States Patent and Trademark Office for her inventions and improvements in cataract surgery. In addition, she received international patents from Japan, Canada, and countries in Europe. Her technique is used around the world. Each year, more than three million cataract surgeries are performed in the United States and more than 10 million worldwide. Patricia's technique has made cataract surgery less painful, more efficient, and more accurate.

BRAINSTORM! Look up each term: ophthalmologist, optometrist, and optician. How are they different?

EXPLORE MORE! To learn more about assistive technology that is available to help those with vision concerns, visit the tech page of the American Institute for Prevention of Blindness at BlindnessPrevention.org/tech.php.

Mark DEAN

{ 1957– }

PERSONAL COMPUTER

These days we take it for granted that we can connect to an external device, such as a printer or keyboard, without any wires. But that was not always the case. Before personal computers could do nearly everything wirelessly, they had to connect to external devices by way of cables.

Because of the work of Mark Dean, a computer scientist, engineer, and inventor, computer users' lives today are much easier. In the 1980s, Mark worked for International Business Machines (IBM), a leader in personal computers. He has more than 40 patents for his inventions. Mark helped to modernize the personal computer that is used in most homes, offices, and schools around the country.

Mark was born in Jefferson City, Tennessee, on March 2, 1957. He attended a segregated school until the third grade when the school districts in Tennessee were integrated. He went to Jefferson City High School and was a straight A student. Mark always enjoyed math and he liked building things. When he was young he and his father built a tractor from scratch.

After high school Mark attended the University of Tennessee at Knoxville. He graduated in 1979 with a bachelor's degree in electrical engineering. Shortly after graduation he was hired by IBM, and he continued his education while working. In 1982, he received a master's degree in electrical engineering from Florida Atlantic University, and in 1992 a earned a doctoral degree in electrical engineering from Stanford University.

In the 1980s, the personal computer (PC) was becoming popular and IBM was an early leader in the field. Mark was part of the team that created and developed the company's first PC. In fact, Mark holds three of the nine patents that IBM received for its original personal computer. He also holds patents for PC additions and upgrades that he invented.

Mark's work at IBM led the way in the development and use of personal computers. The personal computers that were created before the IBM PC didn't really do much. At first, their role was simply to help put information, or data, into mainframe computers. The early PCs had only a few applications but nothing that made people want to use them. The IBM PC changed that. For one thing, because of its smaller size, the new PC could be sold in regular retail stores, where consumers shopped for other things. The Sears, Roebuck and Co. department store chain was one of the early retailers that sold the personal computer. The IBM PC was the first personal computer to be **mass produced** and sold in stores.

The first personal computers only displayed colors in black and white, much like black and white televisions did when they were first developed. In 1981, Mark and his team developed a new technology that made it possible for a PC to create and send a color signal by combining red, blue, and green. The colors were compatible with a television receiver and were designed according to the National Television Systems Committee (NTSC) color system. The NTSC is the standard color system used in the United States and other countries. Mark's technology paved the way for the development of the color PC monitor.

In 1984, Mark and his colleagues invented what's known as the Industry Standard Architecture (ISA) system bus. A bus is a **subsystem** that is used to connect computer components in order to transfer data between them. The ISA system bus that Mark worked to create made it possible for computer users to attach external devices, also known as "peripherals," to their computers.

Peripherals are objects that you connect to a computer to make it do different things. Some are called input devices, such as a computer mouse and keyboard, because they let you interact and control the computer. Some peripherals are called output devices, such as computer monitors, printers, and scanners, because they send information out of the computer and to a peripheral. Still other peripherals function as storage devices.

These include external hard drives and flash drives. All peripherals are extremely helpful in expanding a PC's functions. Some peripheral devices, like monitors, still connect to your computer with a cable, but others, such as your mouse and keyboard, can now connect wirelessly.

In 1999, Mark and his team of engineers created the first gigahertz computer processor chip. A gigahertz is a measurement of how quickly a computer processor can complete a task. The gigahertz chip that Mark developed really sped up the computer—it could process a million calculations every second.

Mark's work at IBM was trailblazing and was key to the company's early success in the personal computer market. In 1999, Mark became the first Black person to be named an IBM Fellow, the highest honor given to a person for technology contributions to the company.

Personal computers are one of the greatest innovations of the 20th century. Because of that innovation, computers are no longer big clunky machines operating in a cold room in an office building. Instead, they are in most homes and on most office desks. Personal computers changed what people did every day and the way things were done. Offices no longer need large file rooms to keep track of all their paperwork. Doctors use them to access their patient information. Teachers use them to conduct lessons, and students use them to do their homework.

The development of the personal computer has led to the development of many other new technologies. For many people, the first step to getting information is by using the computer. If people want information on a company or organization, for instance, they can go to their website. Or, millions of people can now easily access vari-

ous search engines. And because of the mobility of laptop PCs, WiFi technology is everywhere.

Personal computers changed the way people work, learn, and shop around the world. Shoppers are no longer limited to what is close to them. Instead, consumers can purchase items from all over the world, making it possible to find the best prices. According to *National Geographic*, the personal computer is one of the top 10 inventions that changed the world.

BRAINSTORM! What do you think would be a great computer peripheral? What would it do that other products don't, and how might you design it?

EXPLORE MORE! Visit the Computer History Museum in Mountain View, California or online at ComputerHistory.org/timeline to learn about the history of computers and see how they've changed.

Lonnie JOHNSON

{ 1949– }

PRESSURIZED WATER GUN *and* JOHNSON THERMOELECTRIC ENERGY CONVERTER

Some inventors always liked to tinker. Some inventors were always curious about how things work. And some inventors took things apart and put them back together just to see if they could. Then there is Lonnie Johnson. When Lonnie was a young boy he tried to make rocket fuel and ended up setting his family's home on fire. He took his sister's doll apart to see what made the eyes close. And he took scraps that he found in a junkyard, attached them to a lawnmower engine, and made his own go-cart. After a successful career in the Air Force and at the National Aeronautics and Space Administration (NASA), he became an inventor. Lonnie invented a water gun that became one of the best-selling toys in the world, and today he is helping to solve energy problems.

Lonnie was born in Mobile, Alabama, on October 6, 1949. His father, who was a World War II veteran, worked as a driver on a nearby Air Force base. His mother worked as a nurse's aid and in a laundry. During the summer, both of his parents picked cotton on his grandfather's farm. Lonnie had five siblings, and his father taught them all to make their own toys.

When Lonnie was growing up schools in Mobile were segregated. Black kids went to one school, and white kids went to another. Lonnie attended all-Black L. B. Williamson High School. His class was the school's last segregated class. While in high school he was selected to be on the team that represented his school at a junior engineering science fair at the University of Alabama. His was the only Black team at the fair. Lonnie won first place at the fair for his invention of a four-foot-tall, compressed air–powered robot, which he named Linex. Lonnie made Linex out of scraps he found in a junkyard.

Lonnie graduated from high school in 1969 and went to Tuskegee University on a math scholarship. Tuskegee, a historically Black college, was established for Black students when they were barred from attending the same schools as white students. Lonnie received a bachelor's degree in mechanical engineering from Tuskegee in 1973, and two years later he earned a master's degree in nuclear engineering.

After graduating from Tuskegee, Lonnie went into the United States Air Force. While in the Air Force he worked for Oak Ridge National Laboratory, the largest

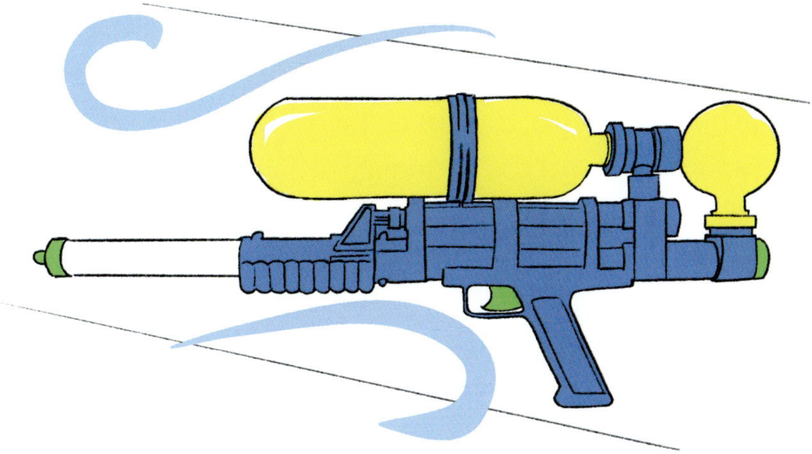

science and energy laboratory run by the United States Department of Energy. Lonnie later worked for NASA in its Jet Propulsion Laboratory.

Over the years, Lonnie never stopped tinkering and experimenting. During his spare time he would work on his many inventions and designs. One evening while he was testing his latest creation, an environmentally friendly heat pump, a gush of water shot out of the nozzle. Although he was surprised by what happened, he immediately thought of how much fun it would be if that could be made into a water gun. Lonnie turned his attention to working on a design. In 1986, he received a patent for his pressurized water gun, which he called a "Squirt Gun." The Squirt Gun has a nozzle, and when the trigger is pulled a continuous flow of pressurized water flows through the nozzle.

In 1989, he sold his invention to the Larami Corporation, a toy company. The company called the toy gun a Power Drencher but later gave it a new name: Super Soaker. The

Super Soaker became extremely popular and sales skyrocketed. The toy water gun that Lonnie invented became one of the top-selling toys in the world. It made billions of dollars for the retail toy industry. One year the water gun was voted the Outdoor Toy of the Year.

That invention and its success inspired Lonnie to create other toys and versions of the water gun. It also inspired him to create a research and development company. Lonnie was on his way to becoming a very successful inventor of toys and other things.

Lonnie made an agreement with Hasbro, a major toy company, to design, engineer, and develop their soft, foam rubber dart guns and other toys made out of foam rubber: also known as the Nerf gun. Those toys soon became very popular. The soft foam rubber toys have made millions of dollars for Lonnie and Hasbro. Over the years, Lonnie went on to file more than 100 patents for his inventions. They include rechargeable batteries, battery parts, heat engines, circuits, and projection systems.

In 2003, a **Nobel Prize Laureate** was asked to do a study to determine the top 10 problem areas facing humanity. His list included population, democracy, education, disease, terrorism and war, poverty, the environment, food, and water. At the top of the list was energy. It was his belief that if the energy problem could be solved the solution to the other problems would follow. When Lonnie learned of the study he set out to solve the two things that created the energy problem: the need for energy and the impact the use of energy has on the environment.

Lonnie's solution to the energy-shortage problem is the Johnson Thermoelectric Energy Converter (JTEC). The JTEC converts thermal energy (heat) into electrical energy. The JTEC could be Lonnie's greatest and most impactful invention. The JTEC was designed to collect energy from the sun and turn it directly into electricity. It uses a one-step process, which is an advancement from other conversion processes that need multiple steps to convert heat to energy.

Lonnie and his team believe that the JTEC will someday become a global leader in clean energy. It is more efficient than solar cells and can be delivered more cheaply. JTEC does not have any moving parts, so maintenance and maintenance costs can be minimized. Also, the price is competitive, which gives it a strong argument for reducing the use of **fossil fuel**. The potential for the JTEC is huge.

BRAINSTORM! Do you agree that energy is the biggest problem for humanity? If yes, explain why. If no, what do you think the biggest problem is?

EXPLORE MORE! To learn more about energy—where it comes from and how it's used—visit the US Energy Information Administration's Energy Kids website at EIA.gov/kids.

Lisa GELOBTER

{ 1971– }

COMPUTER TECHNOLOGY *and* WEB ANIMATION

When Lisa Gelobter enrolled in Brown University, she decided to get a degree in computer science. It wasn't because she had a strong interest in science or computers. She wanted a skill that would keep her employed, so she would never have to worry about paying her bills. Fortunately for the world, she became an exceptional computer scientist. Lisa was instrumental in developing a lot of the technology that people rely on today, including Shockwave, which was important for computers, tablets, smart TVs, and other digital devices.

Lisa was born in 1971 and grew up in New York City. She did not have a lot growing up, but she was committed to completing her education and creating a better life for herself. At Brown, she was a low-income student at a prestigious school. She had to work full-time to support herself and pay her tuition.

Lisa studied as hard as she worked. She concentrated on studying artificial intelligence and machine learning. Artificial intelligence (AI) is the technology that teaches computers, or computer programs, to think like a human. Machine learning is a branch of artificial intelligence. AI is the study of **algorithms** that allow computer programs to automatically improve through experience.

Lisa enrolled at Brown in 1987 but didn't graduate until 2011. It typically takes a full-time student four years to complete their studies and get a bachelor's degree. It took Lisa 24 years to get her degree. But she persisted and never gave up. Lisa calls herself a unicorn because so few Black women earn degrees in computer science. She is pleased that things are changing, and more women and minorities are interested in STEM.

Lisa has worked on internet technology for more than 20 years. She is a digital expert and a highly sought after speaker on technology. Among her accomplishments, she is responsible for developing Shockwave, a computer technology that made the internet fun.

According to Lisa, Shockwave made the web "move." Shockwave was a multimedia platform that people used to play interactive video games on computers. It also allowed people to see video clips as they read articles. Introduced in 1995, it brought animation to the web and soon became the leader in web animation. It made the internet more than a place for information. (Shockwave is now discontinued.)

Lisa is also responsible for developing the technology for animated GIFs. Animated GIFs are image files that have movement. Though they do not have sound, GIFs add emotions to emails and text messages.

Lisa has worked with companies to help them develop videos and their online presence. As the chief digital officer for Black Entertainment Television (BET), she grew the company's digital presence and produced the first live game show in a mobile app. BET is a leading provider of media and entertainment for Black audiences around the world. Further, Lisa was behind the launch of Hulu, a streaming service that offers live and on-demand TV shows and movies. The online video business has grown so much that many people no longer have televisions. Online video is a billion-dollar business, and videos can now be viewed on computers, phones, and tablets. Lisa played a large part in simplifying that process and making the content available to everyone.

Lisa is passionate about using technology to solve difficult problems. She believes that if technology can send a person to outer space, it can be used to solve difficult problems at home, especially those that affect the **disenfranchised**.

When Barack Obama was president, Lisa served as the chief digital service officer at the Department of Education. She used her expertise in technology to provide better service to students at all levels. Under her leadership the department launched College Scorecard, a consumer web app. College Scorecard provides information on colleges and universities to help students and their parents determine the best schools to apply to. The app ranks schools by things such as tuition costs, student loans, and graduation rates. Previous rankings were usually by prestige and alumni donations.

Lisa also believes that technology can be used to address problems in the workplace. That was the basis for forming tEQuitable, her own company. tEQuitable provides a way for employees to speak up anonymously when there are problems at work. Employees can talk about unfair things like bias, discrimination, and harassment. The information they share is confidential, or private, which makes it easier for employees to share their experience. It also helps company leaders fix problems within their organization without connecting a problem to a specific person. More importantly, it lets the leadership know that their organization has a problem and that they need to improve the work environment for the employees.

The impact of some of the technology that Lisa has created and developed is massive. Before web animation, websites were dull and boring—they would just have words on a page. Now web animation is everywhere on the internet. Companies use animation in their online advertising to encourage buyers to make purchases. Schools use it to show what life is like on their campus to attract students. Web animation is so huge and important that companies compete to create their own platforms for users to view web animation.

The ascent of online video is also vast. Online videos were once just for entertainment. Today they are used by businesses and organizations around the world. Online videos are used to teach classes, and they are used to catch up on TV shows, news, and sports events you miss. The online video industry today is a $6 billion industry. Lisa is proud to be a part of that, and she is very proud to be a Black woman in STEM. The internet technologies that Lisa worked to develop and those that followed have become a way of life for most people around the world.

BRAINSTORM! How have online videos changed your life at home and in school? How are you using web animation?

EXPLORE MORE! Visit the College Scorecard website at CollegeScorecard.ed.gov and have fun looking at colleges that you might like to attend one day and at career paths to see what education you will need to apply.

Shirley JACKSON

{ 1946– }

TECHNOLOGY FOR CALLER ID *and* CALL WAITING

When Shirley Jackson was rejected by white students in her first year at the Massachusetts Institute of Technology (MIT) she was hurt and upset, but just for a little while. She stayed focused, concentrated on her studies, and went on to become the first Black woman to receive a doctorate degree from MIT. Shirley became a great scientist and physicist. She has been honored as a leader in innovation and has received numerous science awards. Shirley conducted important research in telecommunications and is responsible for developing the technology that led to Call Waiting and Caller ID.

Shirley was born in Washington, DC, on August 6, 1946. Her father was a World War II veteran and was at **Normandy** on **D-Day**. During the war her mother worked in a factory. With so many men fighting in Europe, factories in the US were left with a need for employees.

Many women answered the call for employees and went to work to produce goods that soldiers needed and to support their families.

Shirley's parents read a lot, which inspired her and her siblings and made them read more. Shirley said there were evenings when the whole family would just sit in a room, reading different things. One person would be reading a newspaper and others would be reading a novel or magazine. Her mother would most likely have been working on a crossword puzzle.

Shirley's interest in science began when she was a young girl. She would catch the bumblebees buzzing around the flowers and shrubbery in her backyard, put them in a jar, and study their actions. Her parents supported and encouraged her interest in science.

Two major historical events also played a role in the direction Shirley's life would take. The first was the United States Supreme Court's decision in the case of *Brown v. Board of Education*. In its historic decision, the court ruled that racial segregation in public schools was unconstitutional. For Shirley that meant more opportunities for a good education. The second event was the launch by the Soviet Union of the Sputnik spacecraft into outer space in 1957. Suddenly there was a lot of interest in science. The United States followed up by making more money and programs available for science education in schools.

Shirley attended Roosevelt High School in Washington, DC. She graduated in 1964 as the class valedictorian and headed to MIT in Cambridge, Massachusetts. It was the vice principal for boys at Roosevelt who suggested that she apply to MIT. Shirley studied physics at MIT for nine years. Much of her time was spent alone, because the white students were not welcoming and refused to work and study with her. When Martin Luther King Jr. was assassinated it lit a spark in Shirley. She decided to help bring more minority students to the school. She also helped to create a Black Students Union in order to bring the school's Black students together for social and political activities.

Shirley graduated from MIT in 1973 with a PhD in **theoretical elementary particle physics**. After graduation, she began working in science laboratories, where she conducted experiments that led to advances in telecommunications. Findings from her research and experiments were used by other inventors to create fiber-optic cables. Fiber-optic technology uses pulses of light, traveling through strands of glass or plastic fibers, to transmit information. Fiber-optic cables are able to cover a wider area than wired cables, and they can transmit much more information. This gives homes and businesses, particularly those in rural areas, better online access. Shirley's contribution to the development of technology for telecommunications is extremely significant. The invention of fiber-optic cables improved the internet, cable television, and telephone systems.

Shirley also developed the technology that makes Call Waiting and Caller ID possible. Both of these technologies help businesses improve their interactions with customers. Since Caller ID identifies the caller, customer service agents know immediately who is contacting them. They can quickly access the customer's records and purchase history, for instance, and direct them to the person who is best able to assist them.

Caller ID has become an important and useful feature for home telephone use as well. As the number of people working from home increases every year, the Caller ID feature allows people to tell if an incoming call is personal or work related. Caller ID works with cell phones, too, identifying the person who is calling.

The Call Waiting feature ensures that a caller never hears a busy signal, which can be especially frustrating for business customers. With the Call Waiting feature, callers don't have to hang up and keep calling back. Instead, the feature puts the caller in line or in a hold position until the person on the other end is able to take their call.

Over her career, Shirley and her work has been widely recognized, including by US presidents. She advised President Bill Clinton on nuclear safety and President Barack Obama on the science needed for manufacturing. In 2008, she received an award for bringing attention to the contributions women have made in science. And in 2016, President Obama awarded her the National Medal of Science, the country's highest honor for achievements in that field.

While Shirley's technological developments improved telecommunication for consumers and businesses, her greatest impact and contribution to science may be her work as the president of Rensselaer Polytechnic Institute, a private university in New York. Under her leadership, she has turned Rensselaer into a top technological research university. Shirley has also spearheaded research on issues that affect humanity, including energy, water, food security, national security, health, and climate change.

Shirley has always worked to bring more women and minorities into STEM. As more and more scientists retire, Shirley is concerned there will be a void, and fewer people will be working on technological and scientific advances. Her goal is to get more students interested in careers in STEM, so that there will not be a shortage of scientists and innovators in the future.

BRAINSTORM! What feature would you like to see added to phones?

EXPLORE MORE! Telephones and their features have changed over the years. Visit the Smithsonian's "Telephones through Time" exhibit at SI.edu/spotlight/phones and have a look at old phones.

Marian CROAK

{ 1955– }

ADVANCES IN VOICE OVER INTERNET PROTOCOL

When Marian Croak was a little girl she was fascinated with repair persons. Whenever they came to her home to fix something, she would follow them around and ask a lot of questions. She was amazed by how they could listen to a pipe or look at an electrical wire and know what they needed to do to fix them. She wanted to be able to do that, and she grew up with a desire to change things and make them better. Indeed, that's what she did. Now she has more than 200 patents for technology inventions. Most of them are for advances in Voice over Internet Protocol (VoIP).

VoIP technology allows people to have phone calls over the internet. According to the United States Patent and Trademark Office, Marian's inventions "made phone calls more reliably and securely transmittable over the internet." She is one of the inventors included in their set of collectible cards featuring the country's greatest inventors.

Marian was born in Pennsylvania in 1955. She grew up in New York City, where she first attended a Catholic high school and later transferred to a public high school. She loved the public school. The teachers there, along with her parents, inspired her and encouraged her love of math and science. Her father, who was uncertain about her attending a public school, became so excited about how well she was doing that he built her a chemistry lab in their home. Marian jokes that he would look away when her experiments went wrong.

After high school, Marian attended Princeton University in New Jersey. She went on to study at the University of Southern California, where she received a PhD in quantitative analysis and social psychology. Quantitative analysis is now called data science.

Marian began her career in technology at AT&T Bell Laboratories in 1982, working on messaging applications. She worked with the team that convinced AT&T to move away from technology that required a physical connection—telephone lines—and move toward communicating over the internet, which she believed was the future.

When the popular TV show *American Idol* started airing on television in 2002, Marian had to watch it every week. It was part of her job. Millions would call in each week to vote for their favorite contestant. It was up to Marian to oversee the call-in procedure and make

sure the calls were routed properly. During one of the shows, she came up with the idea of creating a text-to-vote system. Voting could then take place by two means, either by phoning in or by sending a text message. Text messaging was not very popular at the time, and many people learned about it because of *American Idol*. It soon took off, easing the burden on the phone lines.

Marian has received several patents for technology she invented while working at Bell Laboratories. In 2005, she invented "text-to-donate" technology in response to the damage and destruction caused by Hurricane Katrina. Marian thought that if people could text their donations, the money could be processed much faster than donations made by check or credit card. Katrina was one of the worst hurricanes to hit the United States. More than 1,800 people died in the storm and millions were left homeless in New Orleans, Louisiana, and along the gulf coast of Mississippi. The nation rallied behind the victims and sent donations to organizations that were helping the victims.

Marian's technology was inspired by a desire to speed up the process of getting money as fast as possible. With text-to-donate, mobile phone service carriers would allow their customers to set an amount they wanted to give to a charitable organization. The phone company would add that amount to the customer's bill and then forward the donation to the charity. The action on the customer's end was very simple. With just a few clicks on their cell phone, people could text an amount to a number the charity provided. The American Red Cross, for example, used text-to-donate in 2005 and raised more money than they ever had. Marian's invention forever transformed the way donations are made.

When technology as groundbreaking as VoIP is invented, many scientists and engineers are needed to fully develop and improve it. Marian was a leader in VoIP, and she created some of its greatest improvements. One such improvement is the development of voice recognition technology for accessing teleconferences.

Teleconferences and videoconferences are a major way to conduct meetings and training sessions today. Instead of being in the same location, participants communicate using technology. Many people find themselves having to conduct business remotely, sometimes even from a moving vehicle. If a person is driving, however, it's important to pay attention to the road and not look at a keypad. Marian's invention allowed participants to use their voice to sign in for a teleconference or a videoconference.

In 2013, Marian was inducted into the Women in Technology Hall of Fame. That same year, she won the Thomas A. Edison Patent Award for her text-to-donate technology. Text-to-donate continues to grow and as of August 2019 it was the second-most popular method of donating. VoIP use is also growing every day. Companies all over the world use it. It has made working remotely much easier, because all interaction is done via the internet. And since it is much more affordable than traditional phone lines, VoIP technology has given smaller businesses as well as new businesses the ability to expand their reach globally.

BRAINSTORM! Text is used in lots of different ways, including to donate. How did the text feature improve cell phones, or did they?

EXPLORE MORE! To learn more about the history of telecommunications visit The Connections Museum Denver or The Connections Museum Seattle, or visit them virtually at TelcomHistory.org.

Glossary

abolitionist: a person who was against slavery

algorithm: a procedure for solving a problem or determining something using computer calculations

amputee: a person who has lost a limb such as an arm or leg

assistive technology: equipment, software, and other technologies that help people with disabilities function better

closed-circuit TV: a video system that is used to watch people or actions

D-Day: the day during World War II when the United States and its allies invaded France

disenfranchise: to take away a person's right to vote

enfranchisement: giving someone the right the vote

ephemeris: a table or chart with predictions on the position of the sun, moon, and stars

first responders: the first people to arrive when there is an emergency or disaster

forensic science: science used in solving crimes

forerunner: person or thing that came before another

fossil fuel: carbon containing fuel such as coal and petroleum

groundbreaking: the beginning of something new

high tide: when ocean or sea water is at the highest level

hypocrite: a person who pretends to be something they are not

indentured servant: a person who has to work without pay in exchange for lodging, food, and travel

labor union: a group of workers who join together to fight for and protect their rights

literacy test: a test Black people were forced to take before they could vote

low tide: when ocean or sea water is at the lowest level

mass produce: manufacture large quantities

multigenerational: more than one generation, such as child, parents, and grandparents, living together

multipurpose: having more than one use

Nobel Prize Laureate: someone honored for a great achievement

Normandy: a region in France

poll tax: a tax a person had to pay before they could vote

racially segregated: people separated by race or the color of their skin

residency: the period when a doctor trains and concentrates on one type of medicine

socioeconomic: related to things like a person's wealth, education, and income

solar eclipse: when the sun is blocked by the moon

subsystem: a system that functions as part of a larger system

synthetic: artificial

theoretical elementary particle physics: study of the laws that govern the universe

transfusion medicine: a branch of medicine that focuses on providing blood and its components to patients

tuberculosis: a disease that affects the lungs

working class: people who work in jobs that do not require special skills

Select References

AAE Speakers. "Lisa Gelobter." Accessed December 24, 2020. AllAmericanSpeakers.com/celebritytalentbios/Lisa+Gelobter/396614.

ACS Chemistry For Life. "Charles Richard Drew 'Father of the Blood Bank'." Accessed December 12, 2020. ACS.org/content/acs/en/education/whatischemistry/african-americans-in-sciences/charles-richard-drew.html.

ACS: Chemistry for Life. "George Washington Carver." Accessed December 7, 2020. ACS.org/content/acs/en/education/whatischemistry/landmarks/carver.html.

American Institute for the Prevention of Blindness. Accessed December 27, 2020. BlindnessPrevention.org/index.php.

APS Physics. "Shirley Ann Jackson." Accessed December 30, 2020. APS.org/careers/physicists/profiles/sjackson.cfm.

Bagley, Mary. "George Washington Carver: Biography, Inventions & Quotes." Live Science. December 7, 2013. LiveScience.com/41780-george-washington-carver.html.

Baker, Benjamin. "Bessie Blount Griffin (1914–2009)." BlackPast. October 21, 2018. BlackPast.org/african

-american-history/bessie-blount-griffin-1914-2009.

BDO Black Doctor.Org. "Dr. Marian Croak: Creator of VoIP, The Technology Behind Skype, SMS Messaging & More." Accessed December 26, 2020. BlackDoctor.org/dr-marian-croak-creator-of-voip-the-technology-behind-skype-sms-messaging-more.

Bellis, Mary. "Lyda Newman Invents Vented Hair Brush." ThoughtCo. January 29, 2019. ThoughtCo.com/inventor-lyda-newman-1991285.

Benjamin Banneker Historical Park and Museum. Accessed December 16, 2020. FriendsofBenjaminBanneker.com/park-info/exhibitions-and-collections.

Biography.com editors. "Benjamin Banneker Biography." Updated January 7, 2021. Biography.com/scientist/benjamin-banneker.

Biography.com editors. "Garrett Morgan Biography." The Biography.com Website. Accessed December 13, 2020. Biography.com/inventor/garrett-morgan.

Biography.com editors. "Lyda Newman Biography." The Biography.com Website. Last updated June 22, 2019. Biography.com/activist/lyda-newman.

Biography.com editors. "Mark Dean Biography". The Biography.com Website. Last Updated January 15, 2020. Biography.com/inventor/mark-dean.

Block, Niko. "Elijah McCoy." The Canadian Encyclopedia. Last edited March 1, 2019. TheCanadianEncyclopedia .ca/en/article/elijah-mccoy.

Boyd, Herb. "Inventor Sarah E. Goode, The First Black Woman Awarded a Patent." Accessed December 3, 2020. *Amsterdam News*, July 14, 2016. AmsterdamNews.com/news/2016/jul/14/inventor -sarah-e-goode-first-black-woman-awarded-p.

Brown University. "Harnessing Tech to Power Social Impact with Lisa Gelobter | Thinking Out Loud. April 25, 2015. YouTube. Accessed December 25, 2020. YouTube .com/watch?v=uGqBqAvpU3c.

Cabera, Claudio E. and Jacobs, Julia. "Seven Black Inventors Whose Patents Helped Shape American Life." *The New York Times*, February 24, 2019. NYTimes.com /2019/02/24/us/black-inventors.html.

Case Western University: Encyclopedia of Cleveland History. "Morgan, Garrett A." Accessed December 9, 2020. Case.edu/ech/articles/m/morgan-garrett.

Changing the Face of Medicine. "Dr. Patricia E. Bath." Accessed December 21, 2020. CFMedicine.nlm.nih .gov/physicians/biography_26.html.

Charles R. Drew University of Medicine and Science. "Charles R. Drew, MD." Accessed December 10, 2020. CDrewU.edu/about-cdu/about-dr-charles-r-drew.

Coen, Ross. "Lisa Gelobter" BlackPast, September 19, 2020. BlackPast.org/african-american-history/lisa-gelobter-1971.

Diaz, Sara. "Mark Dean." BlackPast, March 6, 2007. BlackPast.org/african-american-history/dean-mark-1957.

"Elijah McCoy." National Inventors Hall of Fame. Accessed March 19, 2021. Invent.org/inductees/elijah-mccoy.

Eschner, Kat. "This Prolific Inventor Helped Give Us the Phrase "The Real McCoy." *Smithsonian Magazine,* May 2, 2017. Accessed November 23, 2020. SmithsonianMag.com/smart-news/prolific-inventor-helped-give-us-phrase-real-mccoy-180963059.

Essington, Amy. Sarah E. Goode (c.1855–1905). BlackPast. November, 5, 2010. BlackPast.org/african-american-history/goode-sarah-e-c-1855-1905.

Famous Women Inventors. "Lyda Newman: Inventor of an Improved Hair Brush." Accessed December 13, 2020. Women-Inventors.com/Lyda-Newman.asp.

Fox, Janelle Staff Sgt. "Garrett Augustus Morgan: Man behind the mask." Hurlburt Field. January 28, 2013. Hurlburt.af.mil/News/Commentaries/Display/Article/206248/garret-augustus-morgan-man-behind-the-mask.

Genzlinger, Neil. Dr. Patricia Bath, 76, Who Took on Blindness and Earned a Patent, Dies. *The New York Times Obituary,* June 4, 2019. NYtimes.com/2019/06/04/obituaries/dr-patricia-bath-dead.html.

Glover, Steven. "Patricia Bath and the Laserphaco Probe." LaserChirp, February 24, 2016. LaserChirp.com/2016/02/patricia-bath-and-the-laserphaco-probe.

Google Developers. "Women Techmakers Mountain View Summit 2017: Keynote Speech." YouTube. Accessed December 26, 2020. YouTube.com/watch?v=PPwwxIN6M9w.

Hardawar, Devindra. "Mark Dean designed the first IBM PC while breaking racial barriers." engadget February 6, 2015. Engadget.com/2015-02-06-mark-dean-pc-pioneer.html.

Harrison, Greta. "Sending Your Voice Over The Internet? Some called it a Toy. Not Marian Croak." USC Virterbi School of Engineering. *Viterbi Magazine,* Fall 2020. Accessed January 1, 2021. Magazine.viterbi.usc.edu/fall-2020/alumni/sending-your-voice-over-the-internet-some-called-it-a-toy-not-marian-croak.

Hill, Rebecca. "Marie Van Brittan Brown." BlackPast. April 11, 2016. BlackPast.org/african-american-history/brown-marie-van-brittan-1922-1999.

The History Makers. Accessed December 31, 2020. Da.thehistorymakers.org/stories/2;q=Shirley%20Ann%20Jackson; pg=1;pgS=30.

Johnson, Jennifer. "Marian R Croak." BlackPast, December 25, 2018. BlackPast.org/african-american-history/croak-marian-r-1955.

Johnson, Lonnie. "Inventor, Engineer." Accessed December 23, 2020. LonnieJohnson.com.

Johnson Research and Development. Accessed December 24, 2020. JohnsonRD.com/ie/lj/ljprofile.html.

JTEC. "Thermal to Electrical Energy Conversion. Accessed December 24, 2020. JohnsonEMS.com.

JTEC Energy. "Dr. Lonnie Johnson Ted Talk explains JTEC|TEDx Atlanta." Accessed December 29, 2020. YouTube.com/watch?v=Gy3VCs1zeR8.

Keene, Louis. "Benjamin Banneker: The Black Tobacco Farmer Who the Presidents Couldn't Ignore." The White House Historical Association. Accessed December 16, 2020. WhiteHouseHistory.org/benjamin-banneker.

Kelly, Kate. "Marie Van Brittan Brown: Home Security System Inventor." America Comes Alive! Accessed December 19, 2020. AmericaComesAlive.com /marie-van-brittan-brown-home-security -system-inventor.

Latrobe, John H. B, and Daniel Murray Collection. *Biography of Benjamin Banneker.* Washington, American Negro Monograph Co, 1910. Pdf. LoC.gov /item/73207552.

Lemelson-MIT. "Bessie Blount: Electronic Feed Device." Accessed December 12, 2020. Lemelson.mit.edu /resources/bessie-blount.

Lemelson-MIT. "Elijah McCoy: Automatic Drip Cup: Transportation." Accessed November 27, 2020. Lemelson.mit.edu/resources/elijah-mccoy.

Lemelson-MIT. "Marie Van Brittan Brown: Home Security System." Accessed December 19, 2020. lemelson.mit .edu/resources/marie-van-brittan-brown.

Lemelson-MIT. "Patricia Bath: Laserphaco Probe." Accessed December 23, 2020. lemelson.mit.edu /resources/patricia-bath.

Library of Congress. "Women Suffrage Party Mission Statement." Accessed December 15, 2020. LoC.gov/resource/rbcmil.scrp6011805/?sp=4.

Lynn, Samara. "7 Facts You Should Know About Shirley Ann Jackson." *Black Enterprise*, January 25, 2017. BlackEnterprise.com/seven-facts-shirley-jackson.

McNeill, Leila. "The Woman Who Made a Device to Help Disabled Veterans Feed Themselves-And Gave It Away For Free." *Smithsonian Magazine*, October 17, 2018. SmithsonianMag.com/innovation/woman-who-made-device-help-disabled-veterans-feed-themselvesand-gave-it-away-free-180970321.

National Archives. "Folding Beds-Sarah E. Goode". Accessed December 2, 2020. catalog.archives.gov/id/7560384.

National Railroad Hall of Fame. "Elijah McCoy." Accessed November 23, 2020. NRRHoF.org/elijah-mccoy.

NIH US National Library of Medicine: Profiles in Science. "Charles R. Drew: The Charles R. Drew Papers." Accessed December 10, 2020. Profiles.nlm.nih.gov/spotlight/bg.

NPR. "Black Scientist's Path to Success was Often Lonely." March 4, 2009. NPR.org/templates/story/story.php?storyId=101412303.

Ohio History Connection. "Garrett A. Morgan." Accessed December 9, 2020. OhioHistoryCentral.org/w/Garrett_A._Morgan.

PBS. "Who Made America?" Garrett Augustus Morgan. Accessed December 9, 2020. PBS.org/wgbh/they madeamerica/whomade/morgan_hi.html.

Schaffer, Amanda. "The Remarkable Career of Shirley Ann Jackson." MIT Technology Review, December 19, 2017. TechnologyReview.com/2017/12/19/146775 /the-remarkable-career-of-shirley-ann-jackson.

Science History Institute: Chemistry, Engineering, Life Sciences. "Charles Richard Drew." Accessed December 10, 2020. ScienceHistory.org/historical -profile/charles-richard-drew.

Simpson College. "George Washington Carver." Accessed December 9, 2020. Simpson.edu/dunn-library/archives -special-collections/george-washington-carver.

United States Department of Agricultural National Agricultural Library. "George Washington Carver: A National Agricultural Library Digital Exhibit." Accessed December 9, 2020. NAL.USDA.gov/exhibits /ipd/carver.

The University of Tennessee System. "Tennessee Alumnus: Mark E Dean." Accessed January 2, 2021. Alumnus.tennessee.edu/100-distinguished-alumni /mark-dean.

Ursin, Charisse. "Lyda Newman." BlackPast. October 4, 2020. BlackPast.org/african-american-history/lyda-newman-1885.

Walker Jr., Theodore. *Banneker Almanacs for 1792-1797: Descriptions and Transcriptions, Including Benjamin Banneker's 1791 Anti-Slavery Letter to Thomas Jefferson and Jefferson's Reply*. Kindle, 2020.

About the Author

Kathy Trusty is an independent historian and a Black history educator. She has been conducting Black history presentations, creating displays, and producing Black history programs for more than 20 years. In 2003, she created Black History Ed Zone, a Black history education company that produces a line of products called Black PROPS®. These products are created to simplify the inclusion of Black history in the classroom. Kathy is also a speaker and visiting scholar with Delaware Humanities. In 2020, she published a Black history alphabet book for toddlers and preschoolers.